LIVING LANGUAGE®

Learn Spanish Together: For the Car

A PARENT-CHILD ACTIVITY KIT

Activities by
Marie-Claire Antoine

Spanish by
Nancy Noguera

Edited by
Helga Schier, Ph.D.

LIVING LANGUAGE®, A RANDOM HOUSE COMPANY
NEW YORK

Published by Living Language, A Random House Company, New York, New York.
Member of the Random House Information Group

Random House, Inc., New York, Toronto, London, Sydney, Auckland
www.livinglanguage.com

Printed in the United States of America

Design by Jesse Cohen

Library of Congress Cataloging-in-Publication Data
Noguera, Nancy.
Learn Spanish together: for the car / activities by Marie-Claire Antoine ; Spanish by Nancy Noguera ; edited by Helga Schier.
p. cm.—(Living Language parent–child activity kit)
1. Spanish language—Textbooks for foreign speakers—English. 2. Games for travelers. 3. Creative activities and seat work. I. Antoine, Marie-Claire. II. Schier, Helga. III. Title. IV. Series.
PC4129.E5N64 1998
468.2'421—DC21 97-47434

ISBN 0-609-60650-6
10 9 8 7 6 5 4 3 2
First Edition

Contents

Introduction

Living Language® Learn Spanish in the Car is a fun and effective parent-child activity kit that teaches essential Spanish words and phrases through sixteen exciting and easy-to-prepare activities centered around things you see on the road. Whether you already speak Spanish and want your children to learn it, too, or whether you want to learn Spanish along with your children, this program offers great educational fun and entertainment for the entire family. In Driver's Ed, your kids will learn the Spanish words for the road signs you'll pass; in Treasure Hunt, they'll learn how to read maps; and the numbers on the license plates of passing cars will be used to play auto lotto in License Plates: *¡Buena suerte!*

The complete **Learn Spanish in the Car** package includes this 48-page book and one 60-minute cassette.

The book comes complete with a step-by-step description of all sixteen activities, a two-way glossary, a translation of all songs and rhymes used on the recordings, and one page of removable color stickers. At the beginning of each activity, carefully read the instructions with your children, and gather all the materials necessary to complete the activity. During the activity, follow the step-by-step instructions carefully. Turn on the tape and listen, as the two narrators guide you and your children through singing Spanish folk songs, exercising at the rest stop to the rhythm of a Spanish rhyme, and playing a game of I Spy in Spanish. Without even noticing it, you and your children will learn the most essential Spanish words and phrases. Suggestions for adapting and modifying the activity to increase learning conclude every activity.

The book doubles as a scrapbook that your children can personalize with drawings, photographs, or the included stickers to create a record of the completed activities.

The appendix features a two-way glossary that will prove to be an invaluable reference tool. The recordings feature vocabulary, phrases, songs and rhymes, while the two narrators, Juan and Lola, gently lead you and your children through each activity. They'll teach the vocabulary and phrases and provide ample opportunity to practice your pronunciation. Just listen and repeat, and Spanish will easily roll off your tongue. Spanish songs and rhymes help with learning. Don't worry if it seems difficult to follow the songs the first time around. Just rewind to listen to them again. For your convenience, the transcriptions and translations of the songs and rhymes are included in the appendix.

And now, let's begin! *¡Ahora, vamos a empezar!*

Activities

Time: 15 minutes

Vocabulary and Phrases

hola hello • *me llamo* my name is • *si yo fuera* if I were • *la bicicleta* bicycle • *el coche* car
el autobús bus • *el bote* boat • *el avión* airplane • *el camión* truck • *el taxi* taxi
un vehículo a vehicle • *rápido* fast • *lento* slow

YOU NEED

✔ a pen

1. Hello! Are you worried this car trip is going to be boring? Don't be! With **Learn Spanish in the Car,** you won't want to get out of the car! Not only will you get to play fun games, you will also learn to speak a new language: Spanish. Are you ready? Let's start with a little game called If I Were . . .

2. The rule is simple. First, pick a partner. Then pretend to be a vehicle by announcing "If I were a vehicle, I would be . . ." and describe the type of vehicle you'd be. For example, if you decided that you'd be a bicycle, you say that you have two wheels and a saddle. Without asking any questions, your partner must guess what you are.

3. To make this game even more interesting, let's play it in Spanish. To learn your very first Spanish words, turn on your tape now!

4. Remember all the Spanish words you learned? Use as many of them as possible. Say "*Si yo fuera un vehículo* . . ." and your playmate should answer in Spanish. Don't forget to take turns.

5. Here's a variation. Play the game as described, but instead of pretending to be just any vehicle, pretend to be a specific car. Say "If I were a car . . ." and describe what type of car you would be. Would you be a race car, a convertible, or a jeep . . . ? And can you say "If I were a car . . ." in Spanish?*

6. Now look on the right-hand page. See the drawings? Decide if each vehicle pictured is fast or slow. For more fun, write your opinion next to each drawing. Can you say and write these two words in Spanish? After that, look at the list of vehicles. Check "Yes" for all those you've already used (otherwise check "No"). Do you remember what some are called in Spanish? Write their names in Spanish in the column provided.

*Answer: *Si yo fuera un carro* . . .

FAST or SLOW?

 ______________

 ______________

 ______________

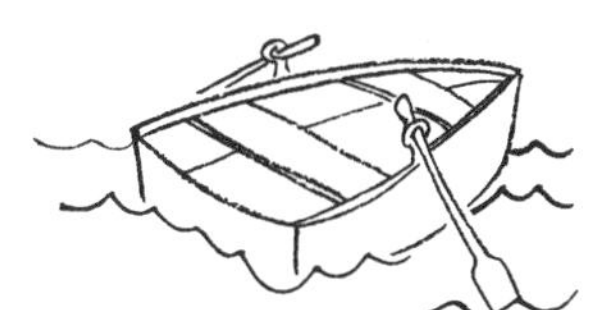 ______________

 ______________

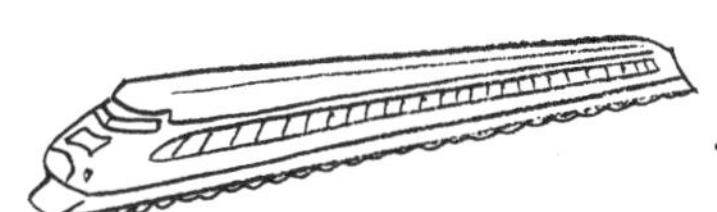 ______________

Have you ever been in . . .

	Yes	No	En español . . .
a boat?	❑	❑	______________
a truck?	❑	❑	______________
a car?	❑	❑	______________
a covered wagon?	❑	❑	una carreta
a bus?	❑	❑	______________
a plane?	❑	❑	______________
a taxi?	❑	❑	______________
a space shuttle?	❑	❑	una nave espacial

Time: 20 minutes

Vocabulary and Phrases

el coche car • *la rueda* wheel • *el motor* engine • *las luces* headlights
el volante steering wheel • *la puerta* door • *la antena* antenna

YOU NEED

- ✔ **stickers for *la rueda* (wheel), *las luces* (headlights), *la antena* (antenna), *la puerta* (car door), *el motor* (engine)**
- ✔ **a pen**

1. Here's a fun activity that will teach you all you need to know about your car!

2. Start by choosing a partner. Take turns naming five things each that are part of your car, inside, outside, or under the hood! Keep taking turns, until you run out of ideas. How long can you keep the game going?

3. Before you start, turn on the tape and listen to some new Spanish words. They will help you play!

4. There's more to this game. First, give yourself five points for each thing you name. But if you name something in Spanish, give yourself twenty points! Compete with your partner to get the most points! Careful: you can't both use the same words!

5. For a variation of the game, pick a "hot letter." What's that? That's a letter you're not allowed to pronounce! It can be part of the word, but you can't say it! For example, if your "hot letter" is "t," you'd say *"la an-ena"* instead of *"la antena."* How do you choose a hot letter? Use the initial of your first name or of your partner's first name. Then play the game as described above. If you pronounce the hot letter, deduct two points from your score. Don't forget: Spanish words give you twenty points (but mind that hot letter!).

6. Now you know all about cars. So let's make sure that the car being built on the right-hand page is complete. On the engineer's notepad, you'll see a list of what's missing. Find the stickers that represent these things, and put them in the right place to complete the car.

My Car

At the car factory

We need:

Time: 5, 10, or 15 minutes

Vocabulary and Phrases

en carro by car • *el carro* car • *la vaca* cow • *el caballo* horse
la oveja sheep • *el perro* dog • *el pájaro* bird

YOU NEED

- ✔ **stickers with *el caballo* (horse), *la vaca* (cow), *la oveja* (sheep), *el perro* (dog), *el pájaro* (bird)**
- ✔ **a pen**

1. You are traveling by car today. What luck! Where are you going? To Grandma's? To a theme park? In any case, you must be anxious to get there. Here's a fun game that will make the trip seem shorter. It's called Animal Spotting. How do you play? That's easy. Look out the car window and watch for animals. For each animal you see, you score points. If you see a sheep, you get five points; for a horse, you get four points; for a cow, you get three points; for a dog, you get two points; and for a bird, you get one point. Spot any other animal and you get a six-point bonus! The winner is the player who reaches a total of thirty points first. As soon as you see an animal, you must say so.

2. Only the first player to spot an animal gets the points. Just say "Cow!" or "Horse!" and score. If you see more than one animal at once, double the corresponding number of points. For example, if you see a herd of eight cows grazing, count six points.

3. Before you start playing, turn on the tape to learn the Spanish names of some animals.

4. Are you ready now? Okay, let's start! Remember: you need at least thirty points to win. To increase the challenge, use your new Spanish words to announce the animals you see.

5. You can also add some variation to Animal Spotting. If there aren't a lot of animals by the side of the road, set a time limit instead of a high score. With your partners, play for 5, 10, or 15 minutes. The player who collects the highest number of points during that time wins the game.

6. You want to play, but you can't see any animals at the moment? Perhaps you are driving in a city or through a tunnel. Be patient. In the meantime, turn on the tape again to learn a fun song: *Juan y Lola tienen una granja* (Juan and Lola Have a Farm).

7. Look at the animals on the right-hand page. Do you remember what they are called in Spanish? Look for the correct stickers and match them with the drawings.

8. Do you like to draw? Use the blank space at the bottom of the page to draw two animals you would find on a farm. Do you know their names in Spanish? What sounds do they make?

What animals are these?

My two favorite farm animals

Time: 15 minutes

Vocabulary and Phrases

ve go • *a la derecha* to the right • *a la izquierda* to the left
derecho straight ahead • *retrocede go* back • *la dirección* direction

YOU NEED

- ✔ **a road map**
- ✔ **a pen**

1. When you are traveling to a new place, how do you find your way? Right, you use a road map. Do you have one in the car? Great! Let's play with it! First, choose a partner. Imagine you are explorers. You are the navigator and your partner is the pilot. Your role is to read the map and guide your partner.

2. Choose a departure point on the map: it could be your hometown or the last city you passed. After that, secretly pick a destination, which is also on the map. The destination can be a city, a forest, a mountain . . . anything that appeals to you!

3. Now guide your partner from the departure point to your secret destination. Give directions (to the right, to the left, straight ahead, backwards) while you both look at the map. Your partner will follow the way on the map according to your instructions. When you stop giving directions, your partner will name the place he or she has reached on the map. Is it your secret destination? If so, switch roles. If not, keep going!

4. One last thing before you start exploring: turn on the tape and learn how to give directions in Spanish.

5. Now that you know all the important Spanish directions, start your game. Pretend you are an explorer from Spain and guide your partner in Spanish.

6. You don't have a map? Or you want more fun but don't want to use the map? Well, let's play Where? Quickly name things you are seeing outside the car window. As you name each thing, your partner will look and say whether you're seeing it to the right, to the left, straight ahead, or behind the car. The faster you name things, the faster your partner has to look and say where those things are. Switch roles when your partner makes a mistake. To make the game more exciting, use the Spanish expressions *a la derecha* (to the right), *a la izquierda* (to the left), *derecho* (straight ahead), and *retrocede* (go back).

7. Still more fun! Look at the right-hand page. Do you see all these tangled lines? Only one leads from your house to Disneyland. Find which one.

Which way to Disneyland?

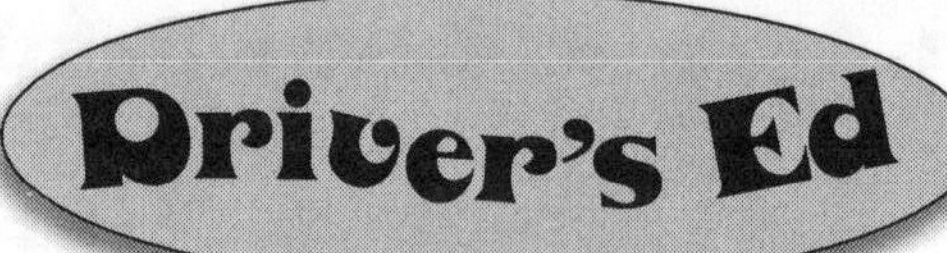

Driver's Ed

Time: 45 minutes

Vocabulary and Phrases

me paro I stop • *sigo adelante* I go forward • *doblo* I turn (I make a turn)
reduzco la velocidad I slow down • *pongo las luces intermitentes* I put the blinker on
paso I pass • *no puedo pasar* I can't pass

YOU NEED

- ✔ **stickers with a stop sign, a deer crossing sign, a speed limit sign**
- ✔ **a pen**

1. Will you learn to drive when you're older? Why not get a head start now? This game is called Driver's Ed. Imagine that you are the driver of your car at this moment. You must pay attention to what's happening on the road and respect the traffic signs. Say which driving decision you make each time you see an actual sign or change on the road. For example, if you see a stop sign, say: "I stop." Or if you see a straight dividing line, say: "I can't pass."

2. Before you "take the wheel," turn on the tape to learn some Spanish driving expressions!

3. To make the game more exciting, pretend you are driving in Puerto Rico. Use as many of the Spanish expressions you learned as you can. Do you remember how to say "I stop" or "I can't pass" in Spanish?

4. You can even be a driving instructor! Choose a partner to be your student, then invent a driving situation for him or her. Your partner will describe what he or she decides to do and mime driving accordingly. For example: say there's a right turn. Your partner will answer "I turn" and mime turning the wheel. Watch your partner! As the instructor, you must catch all the mistakes. Did your student use the blinker? Switch roles after each situation. One more thing: the student is Spanish, so remind your partner to use as many Spanish expressions as possible!

5. Have you noticed any yellow signs on your way? These are warning signs. They may show a picture of men working or children crossing. Look at the right-hand page. See the three blank signs? Read their meaning and invent a picture for each. Be creative!

6. What type of driver would you be? Quick, do the personality test on the right-hand page to find out! Check *Sí* (Yes) or *No* (No) depending on your answer, then read the results. Do you agree with them?

7. More fun? No problem! Find the stickers that represent the road signs described and put them in the right space. What would you do if you saw each sign while driving? Can you say it in Spanish?

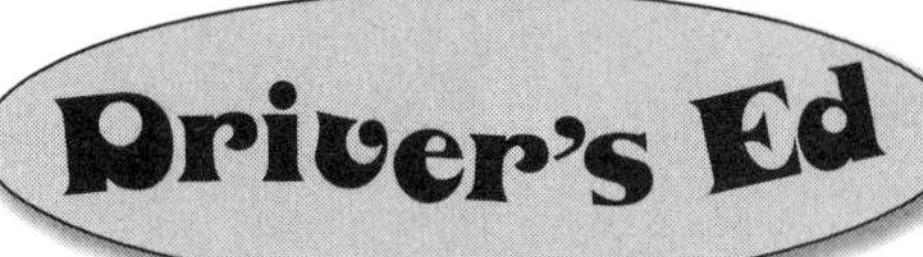

Silly Signs

Draw each sign according to the meaning given.

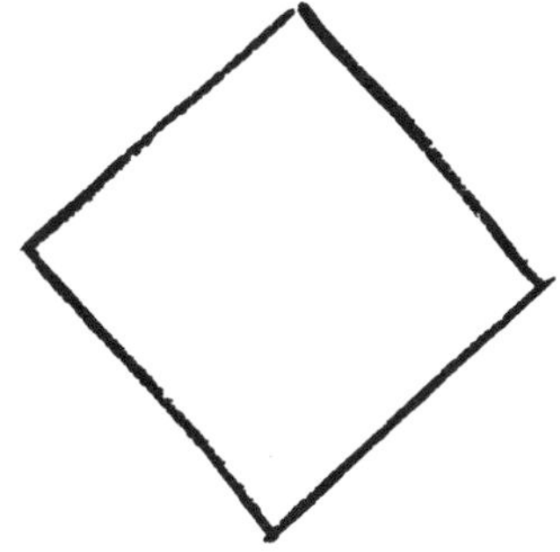

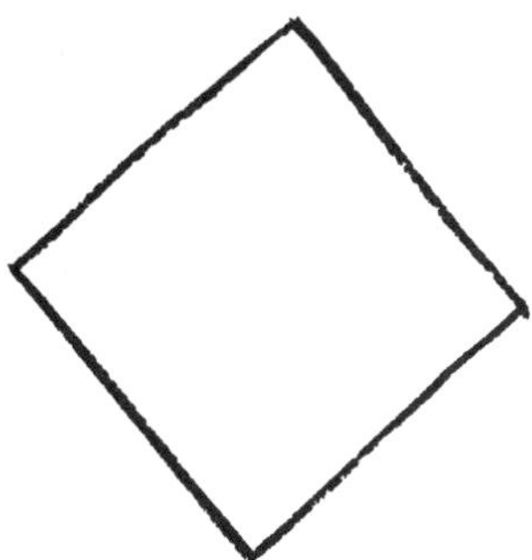

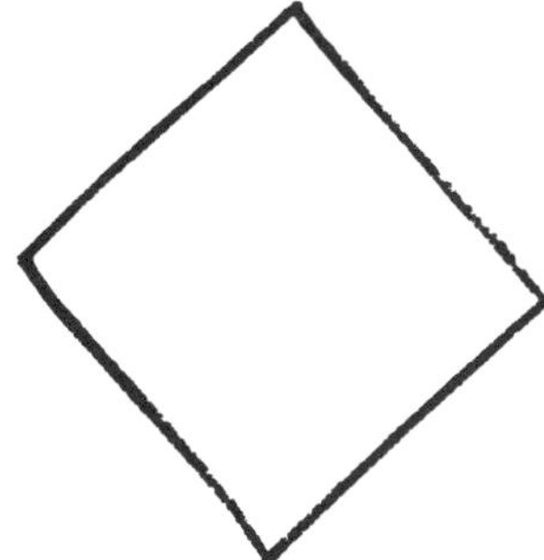

T-Rex Playing

Easter Bunny Working

Speed Limit: 50

Stop

Deer Crossing

What type of driver would you be?

	Sí	*No*
1. The traffic light turns yellow. You stop.	❑	❑
2. You put the blinker on before making a left turn.	❑	❑
3. You slow down when you see the sign for “men at work.”	❑	❑
4. You respect the speed limit.	❑	❑
5. You keep a spare tire in the trunk.	❑	❑

You have a majority of *Sí*. Wonderful! Prudent and aware, you would be a great driver. Your friends would feel safe riding with you!

You have a majority of *No*. Well, it’s a good thing you’re not driving yet! Make sure you learn all the safety rules before you start driving!

On the Road

Time: 30 minutes

Vocabulary and Phrases

la ciudad city • *la escuela* school • *el parque* park • *el zoológico* zoo • *la casa* house
el hotel hotel • *la piscina* swimming pool • *la tienda* shop

YOU NEED

✔ **a pen**

1. What do towns have in common? Each town has houses, schools, and hotels or motels to greet travelers like you. Why not use these places in a game? How? Mime them! First, pick a partner. Then pick one place from the list below. That done, mime what people do there. Act several roles if you need to! For example, if you choose "school" you can mime the teacher and the students. Your partner has to guess which place you chose. He or she will give you the answer in Spanish!

2. Turn on the tape now so you can both learn how to do that.

3. Here is the list of places to choose from:

el parque (park)	*la piscina* (swimming pool)
la escuela (school)	*el hotel* (hotel)
el zoológico (zoo)	*la casa* (house)
la tienda (shop)	

Great! Now, you're ready to play!

4. Here's a variation. Pick a word from the list and say it to your partner. He or she must then mime what one person would be doing there. You have to guess who this person is. For example, if you pick *la tienda* (shop) your partner might mime the salesperson or the customer.

5. Would you like to sing and mime *En el puente de Aviñón* (On the Avignon Bridge), a folk song in Spanish? Turn on the tape now!

6. Look at the right-hand page. There's more fun for you there. Do you remember what these Spanish words mean? Fill in the crossword puzzle with their English equivalents (we wrote one word as an example). When you're finished, the name of a fun place will appear!

7. Now look at the street signs. Their letters got all mixed up by a tornado! Can you put each Spanish word in the right order?

On the Road

Fill in the crossword puzzle with the corresponding English words and find the mystery place*!

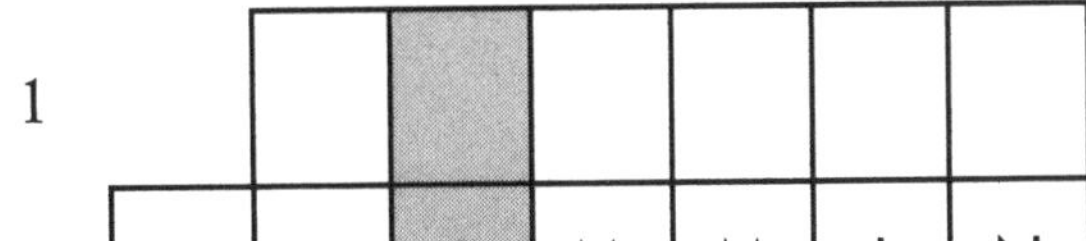

1. escuela
2. piscina
3. parque
4. ciudad
5. casa
6. tienda

1

2 S W I M M I N G P O O L

3

4

5

6

JUMBLE! Unscramble these city signs.†

DANIET

CELUSEA

CANIPIS

SACA

*Answer: *circus.*

†Answer: *tienda, escuela, piscina, casa.*

I'm Hungry!

Time: 25 minutes

Vocabulary and Phrases

tengo hambre I'm hungry • *como* I eat • *esto es* . . . is it . . . • *sí* yes • *no* no
un vegetal a vegetable • *carne* meat • *una fruta* a fruit • *un plato de fast-food* a fast-food dish
postre a dessert • *un helado* an ice cream • *un pastel* a cake

YOU NEED

✔ a pen

1. Are you hungry? What would you like to eat? Let's play food riddles and let your playmates guess! The game is very simple. Pick something you'd like to eat and have your partner guess what it is. Your partner can ask you up to five questions. After that, he or she must guess what you chose. If your partner guesses right, switch roles. *¡Atención!* Answer the questions only with *Sí* or *No*. Do you remember what those words mean? They mean "yes" and "no."

2. Your partner can use some Spanish expressions, too. As a matter of fact, each time he or she asks you a question in Spanish, he or she gets an extra guess at the end! So quick, turn on the tape to learn some food-related expressions.

3. Are you ready? Great! Don't forget to switch roles whenever your partner guesses right. Remember to ask *¿Esto es un(a) . . . ?* (Is it a . . . ?). For example: *¿Esto es un pastel?* (Is it a cake?).

4. Would you like to play another fun food game? Then start by reading this list of food categories:

   • *los vegetales* (vegetables)
   • *la carne* (meat)
   • *los postres* (desserts)
   • *las frutas* (fruits)
   • *los platos de fast-food* (fast-food dishes)

   Choose one category and name as many foods as possible that belong to it. When you can't find another name, the next player takes over. Keep taking turns until everybody runs out of ideas for the category. Can you name some foods in Spanish? Can you say the category in Spanish, too?

5. Look at the right-hand page. Do you see the drawings? How do you feel about each food? Draw a "yummy" sign ☺ if you like that food, or a "yuck" sign ☹ if you don't. When you're done, write the name of the category each food belongs to (fruits, vegetables, meat, etc.). Can you write the categories in Spanish?

6. Imagine you are dining in a Spanish restaurant. After the meal, the waiter brings you the dessert menu. But something is wrong! Read the menu and cross out everything that is not a dessert.

I'm Hungry!

Yummy  **or Yuck**   **?**

 ________  ________  ________

 ________  ________ 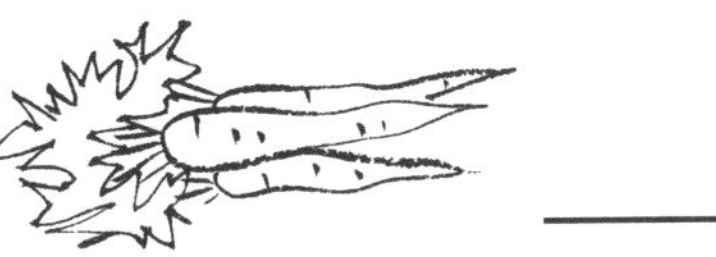 ________

 ________  ________  ________

 ________  ________ 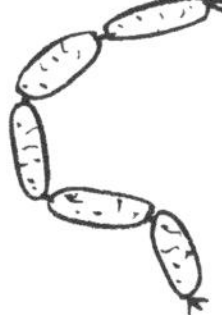 ________

Dessert time!

Cross out everything that is not a dessert.

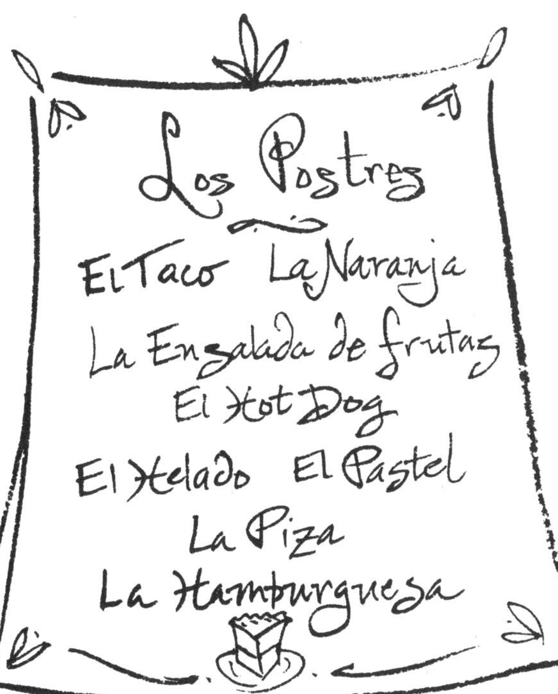

Rest Stop

Time: 15 minutes

Vocabulary and Phrases

Simón dice Simon Says • *¡Baila!* Dance! • *¡Camina!* Walk! • *¡Da la vuelta!* Turn! • *¡Salta!* Jump! *¡Camina de espaldas!* Walk backwards! • *¡Levanta el brazo!* Raise your arm! *¡Levanta la pierna!* Raise your leg! • *¡Aplaude!* Applaud!

YOU NEED

✔ a pen

1. Rest stops are a fun part of the trip. You get to stretch your legs and play. Here's a way to take advantage of that time out of the car: play Simon Says. Do you know this game? First, you need at least one partner. Then choose a game leader. The game leader says "Simon says . . ." and gives a command, like "Dance!" The players must obey and dance. If the game leader gives a command without saying "Simon says" first, the players must not move. If they do, they're out of the game!

2. Now, why don't you make this game more challenging by simply playing it in Spanish? Turn on the tape now to learn the words you will need.

3. Are you ready? Good. Give your first command in Spanish. Of course, you can give commands in English, but try to use as many as possible in your new language. Remember: move only if you hear *Simón dice* . . . (Simon says . . .).

4. How about another game with Spanish commands? Let's play Freeze! In this version, the game leader turns his or her back to the players and gives a command. The players do what they're asked. But as soon as the game leader turns around, they must freeze in whatever position they are in. The first player to move loses!

5. Congratulations! You just got a job at the circus. You are now the elephant trainer. Look at each illustration on the right-hand page. See what the elephant is doing? That's what you ordered him to do. Can you write in each command? Can you write it in Spanish? (We wrote one in as an example.)

The ELEPHANT

BAILA!

License Plates

Time: 10 minutes

Vocabulary and Phrases

uno, dos, tres, cuatro, cinco one, two, three, four, five
seis, siete, ocho, nueve, diez six, seven, eight, nine, ten

YOU NEED

✔ a pen

1. Numbers are written all over your car. They're on the dashboard dials, the radio display, the license plates. . . . Let's play with them. Auto Lotto is like a regular game of lotto, only the numbers you pick must appear on a license plate. Here's what you have to do: Pick three numbers between 1 and 9. Say them out loud, so your parent will know what they are. If two people are playing, it's okay to pick one or two numbers that are the same.

2. For more fun, say your numbers in Spanish. Turn on the tape to learn how to do that.

3. You or your parent will then read the license plate of the next car that passes. How many of your numbers are on it? If your three numbers are part of the car's plate, you win the jackpot! If there are several players, the winner is the one who picked the most numbers on the license plate.

4. Do you want to keep playing with license plates? Look for your birthday! See if your month and date of birth appear on a plate. The player whose birthday appears first wins! And, of course, you can say each number one by one in Spanish.

5. Now look at the right-hand page. One of the numbers in the box is the magic number. To find it, cross out all the numbers that appear more than once. The magic number is the last one left. How do you say that magic number in Spanish?

6. In the blank box, draw the license plate of your car. Don't forget the symbol for your state!

License Plates

Magic number

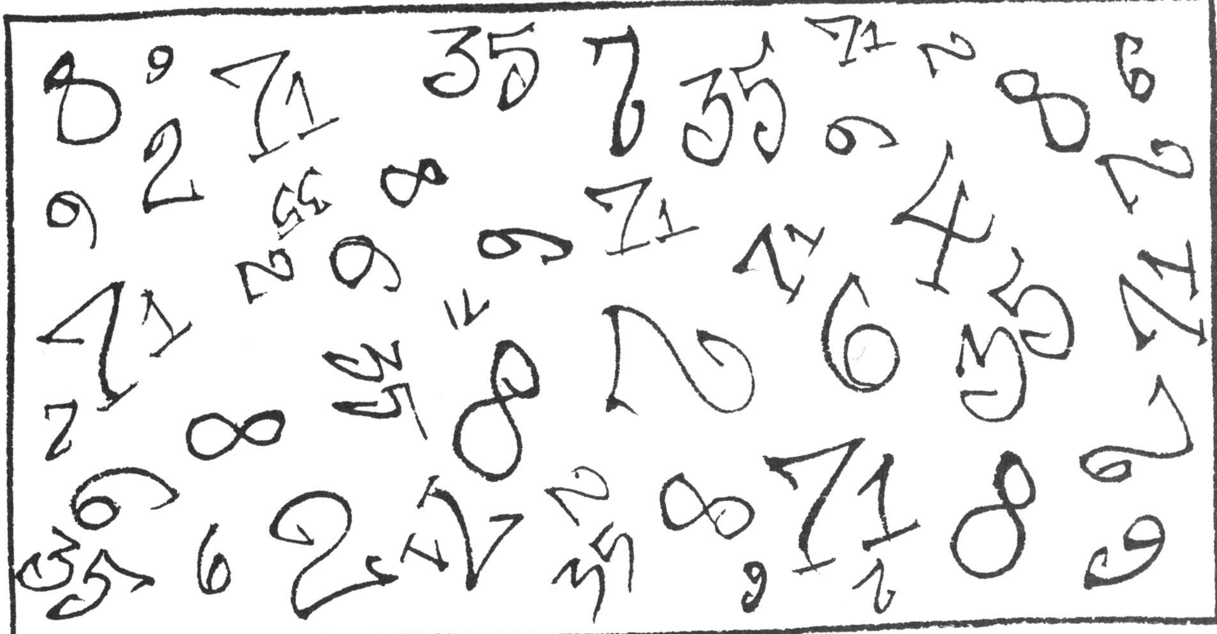

My license plate

Time: 15 minutes

Vocabulary and Phrases

yo canto I sing • *me voy* I'm going • *me voy de viaje* I'm going on a trip • *la canción* song *a cantar* to sing • *el cantante* singer (male) • *la cantante* singer (female) • *el viaje* trip • *papá* dad *mamá* mom • *mi hermano* my brother • *mi hermana* my sister • *la familia* family

YOU NEED

- ✔ **music award sticker**
- ✔ **a pen**

1. Do you like to sing? Great! Let's play Karaoke. Simply sing along with a tape. Which one? Your **Spanish In The Car** tape, of course!

2. First listen to our song. It's called *Bajo el claro de luna* (In the Moonlight). Quick, turn on the tape to learn the words!

3. Now play *Bajo el claro de luna* again and sing along. After ten seconds, your parent will turn off the sound (but not the tape). Keep singing! After a few phrases, your parent will turn the sound back on. Are you at the same place as Juan? Did you sing too fast or too slow? If so, try again!

4. Win a music award! Look for the music award sticker at the end of the book. Then take turns with your playmates singing *Bajo el claro de luna* on your own, without the tape. Your parent will decide who gave the best performance and award the music award sticker to the winner.

5. Now, be a composer! Create a little rap song about your car trip. How? Turn on the tape again. You'll learn a few words you could use in your song and hear an example.

6. Ready? Try to use as many Spanish words as you can in your song. For help, scan this book to find words you've already learned.

7. Now look at the right-hand page. See the letters on the Word Scramble tiles? Which Spanish words can you make with these letters? Here's a hint: You can make four words, all related to the Spanish word for "song."*

8. Finally, draw your family. When you're done, label each person. Can you label everybody in Spanish?

*Answer: *canción, cantar, el cantante y la cantante.*

Word Scramble

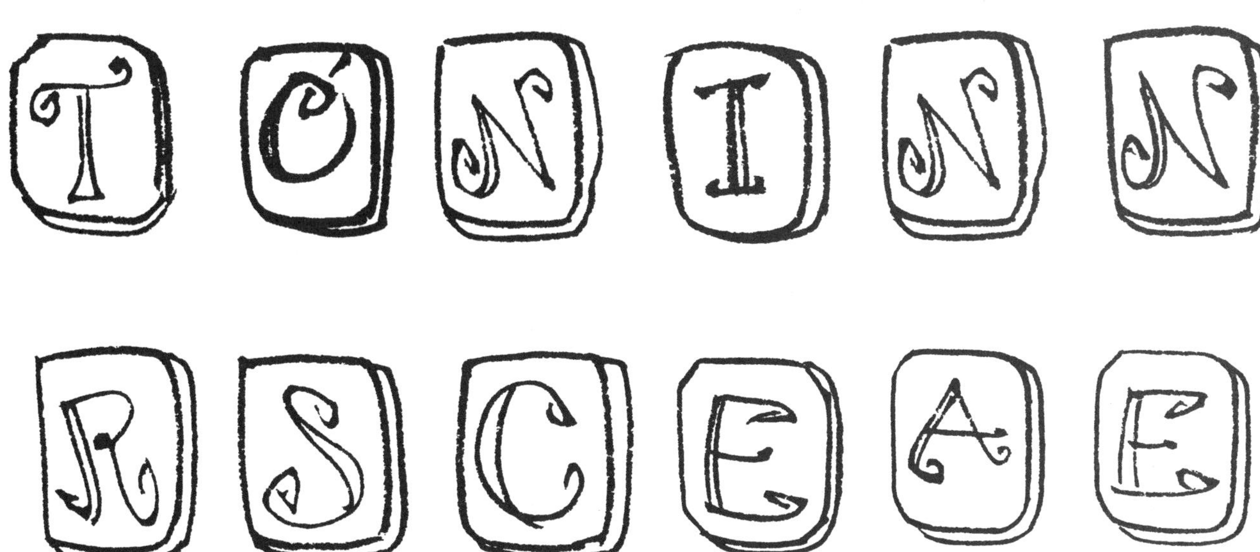

My family

Wild Nature

Time: 30 minutes

Vocabulary and Phrases

la naturaleza nature • *el venado* deer • *el bosque* forest • *el árbol* tree
el animal animal • *la serpiente* snake • *el desierto* desert • *el oso* bear • *el águila* eagle
la montaña mountain • *el tiburón* shark • *el océano* ocean • *el león* lion • *la selva* jungle

YOU NEED

- ✔ **stickers with *el océano* (ocean), *la montaña* (mountain), *el bosque* (forest), *el árbol* (tree), *la selva* (jungle)**
- ✔ **a pen**

1. Are you traveling through a forest? Passing through a desert? Maybe you are rolling up and down mountains or hills? In any case, there are certainly many wild animals living nearby, perhaps big bears or snakes. Even in the city, there are wild animals. Where? At the zoo, of course! Here's a fun game to play. It's called Animal Charades. It's simple. Mime a wild animal and your partner guesses which one it is.

2. First, decide which wild animal you will mime. Then tell your partner where this animal lives. For example, does it live in the ocean or in the jungle? After giving the clue, don't make another sound! Start miming the animal you chose, using only your face and hands. Take turns with your partner after he or she gives the right answer. If you have several playmates, the next turn belongs to the player who first guesses correctly.

3. For even more fun, you can give the clue in Spanish. How? Well, first you need to turn on the tape to learn the Spanish words.

4. If you get tired of being silent, you can imitate the sound of an animal instead of miming it. Give the clue as explained above and start growling, roaring, or whatever! But try not to be too loud!

5. After playing Animal Charades, why not sing a song? *La madre Micaela* (Mother Michaela) is a fun Spanish song. Turn on the tape again.

6. Look at the animals on the right-hand page. Find the stickers that tell where they live in Spanish, and match them with each drawing.

7. Go on a paper safari. Each time you see an animal, write its Spanish name on the right-hand page, draw it, and note in Spanish where it lives and what it eats. Which one would you prefer as a pet? What do your parents think about that?

Wild Nature

Where do they live?

Paper Safari

Animal I saw	Where it lives	What it eats

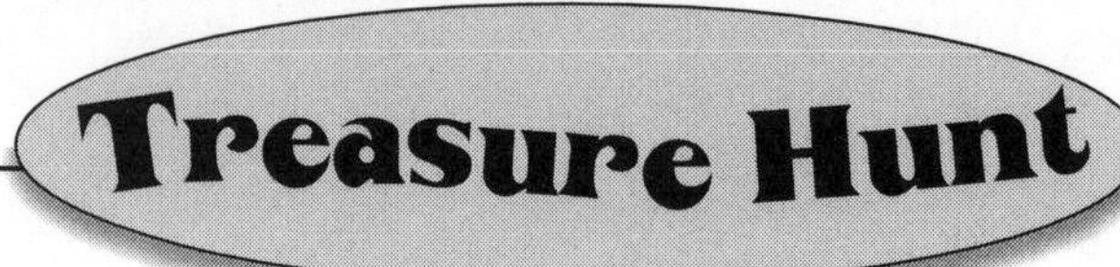

Time: 10 minutes

Vocabulary and Phrases

yo tengo I have • *tú tienes* you have • *la cinta* cassette • *el pañuelo* handkerchief *los lentes de sol* sunglasses • *el sombrero* hat • *la pluma* pen • *el juguete* toy *el juego de video* video game • *el mapa* map • *el libro* book • *la moneda* coin

YOU NEED

✔ **a pen**

1. Are you tired of looking out the window? Well, then, look in the car! There's nothing to see? Not so! There are even enough things for you to go on a Treasure Hunt.

2. The principle of the game is simple. First, choose a partner to play with. Then compete to find as many objects as possible within a short time limit. The objects you need to find are listed below. But first, turn on the tape to learn how to say these words in Spanish.

3. Ready? Here is the list of things you must find:

   el pañuelo (handkerchief)
   el libro (book)
   el juego de video (video game)
   la moneda (coin)
   el sombrero (hat)
   el mapa (map)
   la pluma (pen)
   el juguete (toy)
   la cinta (cassette)
   los lentes de sol (sunglasses)

4. You have five minutes to collect as many of the objects as possible. The first player who sees an object gets it. Your parent can act as a referee in case of disagreement. After five minutes, your parent will tell you to stop. The winner is the player who has collected everything, or the player who has the most points. Count ten points for each object you have. If you name an object in Spanish, count twenty points! So even with fewer objects you could still win if you speak more Spanish than your partner does!

5. Look at the maze on the right-hand page. Can you find the way to the treasure? Look at the objects you pass on your way. Can you give their names in Spanish?

LIBERTY
1976
START

Time: 10 minutes

Vocabulary and Phrases

veo I see • *algo* something • *que comienza con* that starts with
el abcedario español the Spanish alphabet

YOU NEED

- ✔ **stickers with the letters A, V, G, O, P, R, T, W, E, H**
- ✔ **a pen**

1. Are you passing through a city? Wonderful! It's the perfect place to play I Spy. First, look out the window and pick something you are seeing at the moment. Don't tell what it is! Just say "I spy something that starts with . . ." and give the first letter of the word. Your partner then tries to figure out what you spied. He or she will look only for things that start with the letter you gave. When he or she has found it, switch roles.

2. Do you have your spy sunglasses on? Great! To make the game more challenging, give the first letter of the thing you spy in Spanish. Turn on the tape now to learn the Spanish alphabet!

3. Now you're ready. Do you remember how to say "I see something that starts with . . . ?" You say: "*Veo algo que comienza con . . .*"

4. Of course, you don't have to be in a city to play. You can choose something you are seeing along the road, in the car, or even in the car behind you!

5. The Spanish alphabet can also become a secret spy code: use it to spell secret words to your partner. And if you'd like to learn a fun alphabet poem called *El abcedario es una rima* (The Alphabet Is a Rhyme), turn on the tape again.

6. Look on the right-hand page. See the message? It's top secret! Some letters have been erased by accident. Find the stickers with the letters to complete and read this very important message. When you're done, look at the second message. It's coded. To read it, write the letters that correspond to each number. Can you say those letters in Spanish?

Top Secret!

Complete the message with the stickers of the missing letters.

DEAR AGENT 807:

I WILL BE GOING ON A TRIP NEXT SATURD_____Y. I WILL LEA______E EARLY IN THE MORNIN______. PLEASE, MAKE SURE YOU GO TO MY H______USE. (YOU KNOW WHERE IT IS.) MY PET FISH NEEDS TO BE FED. I KNOW YOU ARE WORRIED BECAUSE MY _____ET IS A BIG SHA______K, BUT "TOOTSIE" IS VERY GENTLE. JUST BE CAREFUL WHEN YOU PU______YOUR HAND IN THE _______ATER! I WILL RETURN NEXT W______DNESDAY. T______ANK YOU FOR YOUR HELP.

P.S. TOOTSIE IS IMPATIENT TO SEE YOU!

AGENT 000

Break the code! Write the corresponding letter under each number.

15.4.10.11.10 1.11.10 24.1.2.7 15.4.9.2.14.17 15.21 17.10.10 9.2 1 13.9.15.7

26.18.15 15.4.10 25.9.5.6.10.17.15 8.5.1.13.10 9.17 15.4.10 22.21.21!

Secret code

A=1 B=26 C=13 D=6 E=10 F=19 G=14 H=4 I=9 J=20 K=16 L=5 M=24

N=2 O=21 P= 8 Q=23 R=11 S=17 T=15 U=18 V=12 W=25 X=3 Y=7 Z=22

Colors

Time: 20 minutes

Vocabulary and Phrases

color color • *rojo* red • *blanco* white • *azul* blue • *anaranjado* orange • *gris* gray • *amarillo* yellow *verde* green • *rosado* pink • *violeta* purple • *negro* black • *marrón* brown

YOU NEED

- ✔ **stickers for *rojo* (red), *azul* (blue), *verde* (green), *amarillo* (yellow)**
- ✔ **a pen**

1. Doesn't the road look like a rainbow with all these colorful cars and trucks? Here's a rainbow of activities called Color Me . . . First, choose a partner. Tell him or her: "Color me . . ." and give a color of your choice—in Spanish! Your partner has to name as many things as possible of that color. For example, suppose you say "Color me *verde*" (green). Your partner might answer: "grass, a frog, leaves, my uncle's car, my friend Annie's eyes, my favorite T-shirt, my school bag," until he or she can't think of anything else that's green. At that point, switch roles. Your partner will choose a new Spanish color for you. Who will give the longest answer?

2. Before you find out, turn on the tape so you can learn the Spanish names of the colors and a fun poem called *Los colores del universo* (The Colors of the Universe).

3. Are you up for a challenge? Choose a color as above, but name only things of that color you are actually seeing out of the car window. Compete with your partner by keeping score, counting 10 points for each thing you name.

4. Here's another colorful idea. Name the colors of the next ten cars you pass. Compete with your partner to announce the color first. Can you name the colors in Spanish? The player who gives the most color names in Spanish becomes the "Rainbow Master"!

5. More fun? Pretend you are exploring a new planet. It's very much like Earth, except the colors are different. For example: the sky is red and the grass is purple! Can you imagine that new planet? Imagine the color of its ocean, trees, mountains, sun, moon, snow . . . and everything else you can think of. Be creative! And since you're on a foreign planet, why not use a foreign language? Can you say some of the colors in Spanish?

6. Now, look at the right-hand page. Imagine that you've found old black and white pictures. Read what each picture represents, then place the sticker with the name of its color next to it. When you're done, answer the questions about your favorite colors. Can you write some answers in Spanish?

Colors

What color is each picture?

Bananas

Fire Truck

Ocean

Prairie

What color is . . .

your favorite T-shirt? __________

your car? __________

your favorite hat? __________

your school bag? __________

My favorite color is __________.

My least favorite color is __________.

Every Day's a Holiday!

Time: 10 minutes

Vocabulary and Phrases

hoy es . . . today is . . . • *hoy* today • *el día* day
lunes Monday • *martes* Tuesday • *miércoles* Wednesday • *jueves* Thursday
viernes Friday • *sábado* Saturday • *domingo* Sunday

YOU NEED

- ✔ **stickers with *lunes* (Monday), *martes* (Tuesday), *miércoles* (Wednesday), *jueves* (Thursday), *viernes* (Friday), *sábado* (Saturday), *domingo* (Sunday)**
- ✔ **a pen**

1. What day is today? What did you do yesterday? What are your plans for tomorrow? Turn on the tape to learn the days of the week in Spanish.

2. This game will take you into the past, present, and future! Let's start with today's day. Give it in Spanish. Now think of what happened today and name someone you met, something you ate, something you read, something you played, and something you're wearing.

3. Good! Now do the same thing for yesterday. Give yesterday's day in Spanish, then name someone you met, something you ate, something you read, something you played, and something you wore!

4. That was the present and the past. Can you predict the future? Say what day tomorrow will be and name who you will meet; what you will eat, read, play, and wear! Can you go farther in the future and predict those things for the next weekend? Don't forget to give the name of each day in Spanish!

5. Now look on the right-hand page. There's a calendar that looks very empty! Imagine each day is a holiday. First, find the stickers with the days of the week in Spanish and place them on top, over the corresponding days in English. Then, for each day, write or draw what you would like to do in the morning and in the afternoon. Think of all the things you like to do when you're having a holiday! Have fun!

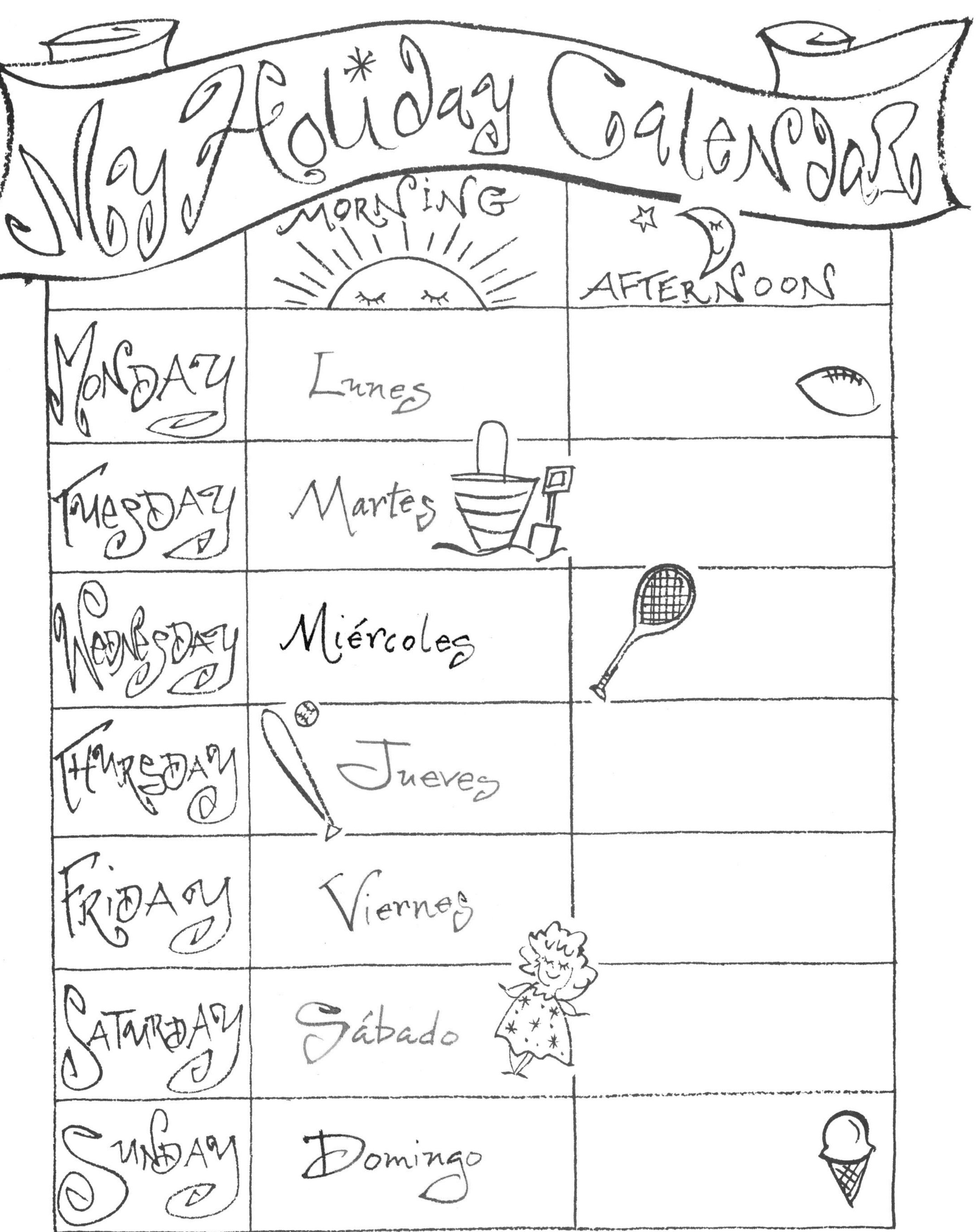

My Holiday Calendar

	MORNING	AFTERNOON
MONDAY	Lunes	
TUESDAY	Martes	
WEDNESDAY	Miércoles	
THURSDAY	Jueves	
FRIDAY	Viernes	
SATURDAY	Sábado	
SUNDAY	Domingo	

We're Here!

Time: 20 minutes

Vocabulary and Phrases

algo something • *es divertido* it's fun • *aburrido* boring • *largo* long • *corto* short • *raro* strange
bello beautiful • *feo* ugly • *grande* big • *pequeño* small

YOU NEED

✔ **a pen**

1. Is your trip almost over? Here's an activity that will help you remember it. Can you remember what you've seen on the way? Can you say if it was fun, boring, or even strange? That's what you'll do with this game.

2. Turn on the tape to learn how to describe things in Spanish.

3. Now pick a partner. Ask him or her one of the questions from the list below. Say: "Name . . ."

- *algo grande* (something big)
- *algo divertido* (something fun)
- *algo feo* (something ugly)
- *algo raro* (something strange)
- *algo pequeño* (something small)
- *algo aburrido* (something boring)
- *algo bello* (something beautiful)

Your partner has to name two things he or she saw during the trip that correspond to what you asked. For example, you may ask: "Name *algo grande.*" He or she might answer: "A mountain and the bridge we just passed."

4. Switch roles after each question. Keep score. Count 10 points for each answer. If you read the question in Spanish, add 20 points to your score. Keep playing until you run out of ideas and can't answer any of the questions! The player who has the most points is the winner!

5. Another challenge? Can you give some of the answers in Spanish? If so, count 50 points for each! To help you, look for Spanish words all through this book.

6. Look on the right-hand page. There's a secret message hidden in the puzzle. To discover it, find all the listed words in the puzzle. Make sure you look carefully in all directions. When you're done, write all the unused letters and read the message!

7. So, how was your trip? Was it fun? Boring? Short? Long? Circle the words that match your opinion, and cross out the others. Look at the words you've circled. Do you remember how to say them in Spanish?

Word Search

All these words are in the puzzle. To find them, look from right to left, left to right, up, down, and diagonally. When you have found all the words, write the remaining unused letters from left to right and see a secret message appear!

AIRPLANE
BACKPACK
BICYCLE
BOAT
BUS
CAMP
CAR
DRIVING

B	H	B	D	R	I	V	I	N	G
U	I	A	I	R	P	L	A	N	E
S	N	C	A	B	P	P	I	R	T
U	I	K	Y	P	O	M	Y	R	H
N	A	P	H	C	O	A	L	O	G
T	R	A	V	E	L	C	T	A	I
A	T	C	A	R	D	E	M	D	A
N	Y	K	T	O	L	E	Y	O	U

GAME
HOTEL
ROAD
SUNTAN
TRAIN
TRAVEL
TRIP

The secret message is: ______________________________.

My trip was . . .

boring **fun**
short **long**
strange **beautiful**

Answer: Happy holiday to you.

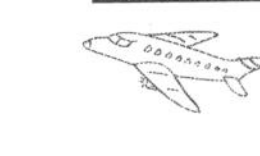

Appendixes

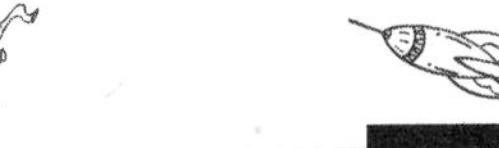

Songs and Rhymes

JUAN Y LOLA TIENEN UNA GRANJA.

Juan y Lola tienen una granja.
tra-la-la-la-la
En la granja tienen una vaca.
tra-la-la-la-la
La vaca dice mu mu.
Y mu, mu, mu, mu.
Ella dice mu, repite mu.
¡Siempre dice mu!

Juan y Lola tienen una granja.
tra-la-la-la-la
En su granja tienen una oveja.
tra-la-la-la-la
La oveja dice ba ba.
Y ba, ba, ba, ba.
Ella dice ba, repite ba.
¡Siempre dice ba!

Juan y Lola tienen una granja.
tra-la-la-la-la
En su granja tienen un perro.
tra-la-la-la-la
El perro dice wuf, wuf.
Y wuf, wuf, wuf, wuf.
Y dice wuf, repite wuf.
¡Siempre dice wuf!

JUAN AND LOLA HAVE A FARM.

Juan and Lola have a farm.
tra-la-la-la-la
On their farm they have a cow.
tra-la-la-la-la
The cow says moo moo.
And moo, moo, moo, moo.
It says moo, repeats moo.
It always says moo!

Juan and Lola have a farm.
tra-la-la-la-la
On their farm they have a sheep.
tra-la-la-la-la
The sheep says bah bah.
And bah-bah-bah-bah.
It says bah, repeats bah.
It always says bah!

Juan and Lola have a farm.
tra-la-la-la-la
On their farm they have a dog.
tra-la-la-la-la
The sheep says bow-wow.
And bow-wow-bow-wow.
It says bow-wow, repeats bow-wow.
It always says bow-wow!

EN EL PUENTE DE AVIÑÓN.

Todos bailan, todos bailan.
En el puente de Aviñón,
Todos bailan, yo también.
Bailan allí, así los caballeros,
Bailan allí y después bailan allá.

Bailan allí, así las lavanderas,

Bailan allí y después bailan allá.

En el puente de Aviñón,
todos bailan, todos bailan.
En el puente de Aviñón,
todos bailan, yo también.

ON THE AVIGNON BRIDGE.

Everyone is dancing, everyone is dancing.
On the Avignon bridge,
everyone is dancing, including me.
They're dancing here, like the gentlemen.
They're dancing here, and then they're dancing there.
They're dancing here, like the washer-women.
They're dancing here, and then they're dancing there.
On the Avignon bridge,
everyone is dancing, everyone is dancing.
On the Avignon bridge,
everyone is dancing, including me.

BAJO EL CLARO DE LUNA.

Bajo el claro de luna, mi amigo Adam,
préstame la pluma para escribirle a tú.

Mi vela se apagó, y ya no tengo luz.
Abreme la puerta, por amor de Dios.

Bajo el claro de luna, Adam respondió:
yo no tengo pluma, en cama estoy.
Vé donde la vecina, creo que está allí.
Porque en su cocina, brilla un candil.

IN THE MOONLIGHT.

In the moonlight, my friend Adam,
lend me your quill pen, so I can write to you.

My candle has died, I have no light left.
Open your door, for goodness' sake.

In the moonlight, Adam answered:
I have no quill pen, I am in my bed.
Go see the neighbor, I think she's home.
Because in her kitchen, someone's striking a light.

LA MADRE MICAELA.

La madre Micaela perdió su gato,
y grita por la ventana que se lo devuelvan.
El padre Lucrecio le respondió:
Ay, madre Micaela, su gato no se perdió.

Al compás de tra la la la,
Al compás de tra la la la.
Al compás de tra de ri de ra tra la la.

MOTHER MICHAELA.

Mother Michaela has lost her cat,
She shouts out the window to get it back.
It was Father Lucretio who answered her:
Come on, Mother Michaela, your cat isn't lost.
To the tune of tra la la la,
To the tune of tra la la la.
To the tune of tra de ri de ra tra la la.

EL ABCEDARIO ES UNA RIMA.

A, B, C, ¿quién es usted?
D, E, F, soy un gran jefe.
G, H, I, ¿qué hace aquí?
J, K, L, vengo a recoger laureles.
M, N, Ñ, O, pero alquién los cortó.
P, Q, R, ¿y qué más quieres?
S, T, U, un amigo como tú
V, W, con los lentes al revés
X, Y, y zapatos en los pies
y la Z, zipizape!

THE ALPHABET IS A RHYME.

A, B, C, who are you?
D, E, F, I am a great chief.
G, H, I, what are you doing here?
J, K, L, I came to pick laurels.
M, N, Ñ, O, but someone cut them up.
P, Q, R, what else do you want?
S, T, U, a friend like you
V, W, with the eye glasses twisted
X, Y, and wearing shoes
And the Z is a fuss!

LOS COLORES DEL UNIVERSO.

Los colores del universo
El planeta Tierra es azul.
El planeta Marte es rojo.
El planeta Júpiter es anaranjado.
La luna es gris,
y el sol es amarillo.
¡El universo es un arco íris!

THE COLORS OF THE UNIVERSE.

The colors of the universe
Planet Earth is blue.
Planet Mars is red.
Planet Jupiter is orange.
The moon is gray,
and the sun is yellow.
The universe is a rainbow!

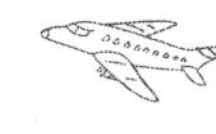

Glossary

Notes

- All Spanish articles, nouns, and adjectives have a gender. They are either masculine or feminine. The article preceding the noun indicates the gender of the noun. *El* (the) and *un* (a) are masculine articles, *la* and *una* are feminine articles. The plural masculine articles are *los*, *unos* and the plural feminine articles are *las*, *unas*.
- To form the plural of most nouns, simply add a final "s" to the noun ending in a vowel. To nouns ending in a consonant, add "es."
- All adjectives agree in gender and number with the noun they modify.

Spanish–English

A

abcedario	alphabet
aburrido(a)	boring
águila	eagle
algo	something
amar	to love
amarillo(a)	yellow
animal (el) (pl. *los animales*)	animal
antena (la)	antenna
aplaudir	to applaud
¡Aplaude!	Applaud!
aplaudo	I applaud
árbol (el)	tree
autobús (el)	bus
avanzar	to go forward
avión (el)	airplane
azul	blue

B

bailar	to dance
¡Baila!	Dance!
bailo	I dance
barco (el)	boat
bello/a(s)	beautiful, pretty
blanco(a)	white
bosque (el)	forest
brazo (el)	arm

C

caballo (el)	horse
caminar	to walk
¡Caminen!	Walk!
camino	I walk
tú caminas	you walk
camión (el)	truck
canción (la)	song
candil	light
cantar	to sing
carne (la)	meat
cinta (la)	cassette
ciudad (la)	city
color (el)	color
coche (el)	car
comenzar	to start
comer	to eat
corto	short

D

decir	to say
digo	I say
"Simón dice . . ."	"Simon says . . ."
derecha	straight
desierto (el)	dessert
detenerse/pararse	to stop
me detengo/paro	I stop
día (el)	day
dirección (la)	direction
divertido(a)	fun
¡Diviertánse!	Have fun!
doblar	to turn, to make a turn
domingo	Sunday

E

él	he, it *(m.)*
ella	she, it *(f.)*
ellas	they *(f.)*
ellos	they *(m.)*
en	in
escuela (la)	school
español	Spanish

F

familia (la)	family
fast-food (el)	fast-food
feo(a)	ugly
fruta (la)	fruit

G

grande	tall, big
gris	gray
gustar	to like
me gusta . . .	I like . . .

H

hambre	hunger
tener hambre	to be hungry
helado (el)	ice cream
hermana (la)	sister
hermano (el)	brother
hola	hello
hotel (el)	hotel
hoy	today

I

intermitente	blinker
ir	to go
izquierda	left

J

juego (el)	game
juego(s) de video	video game(s)
jueves	Thursday
juguete (el)	toy

L

largo	long
lentes de sol (los)	sunglasses
lento	slow
león (el)	lion
levantar	to raise
¡Levanta el brazo!	Raise your arm!
¡Levanta la pierna!	Raise your leg!
libro (el)	book
llamarse	to be called
me llamo	my name is
¿Cómo te llamas?	What's your name?
luces (las)	headlights
lunes	Monday

M

mamá (la)	mom
mapa (el)	map
marrón	brown
martes	Tuesday
miércoles	Wednesday
moneda (la)	coin
montaña (la)	mountain
motor (el)	engine

N

naranja (la)	orange
naturaleza (la)	nature
negro(a)	black
niña (la)	girl
niño (el)	boy
no	no
nosotros	we

O

océano (el)	ocean
oso (el)	bear
oveja (la)	sheep

P

pájaro (el)	bird
pañuelo (el)	handkerchief
papá (el)	dad
parar	to stop
paro	I stop
parque (el)	park

asar	to pass (another car)
astel (el)	cake
eligro (el)	danger
equeño(a)	small
erro (el)	dog
ierna (la)	leg
iscina (la)	swimming pool
lato (el)	dish
luma (la)	pen
oner	to put
or	by
ostre (el)	dessert
uerta (la)	door

Q

ue	what, who, which
que comienza por . . .	that starts with . . .

R

ápido	fast
aro	strange, odd
ebasar	to pass (another car)
rebaso	I pass
tú rebasas	you pass
educir	to slow down
reduzco	I slow down
etroceder	to go back
¡Retrocede!	Go back!
rojo(a)	red
rosado(a)	pink
rueda (la)	wheel

S

sábado	Saturday
saltar	to jump
¡Salta!	Jump!
salto	I jump
se llama	she/he/it is called
selva (la)	jungle
semana (la)	week
ser	to be
soy	I am
tú eres	you are
él/ella es	he/she is
serpiente (la)	snake
si	if
sí	yes
sombrero (el)	hat

T

taxi (el)	taxi
tener	to have
tengo	I have
tienes	you have
tener hambre	to be hungry
tesoro (el)	treasure
tiburón (el)	shark
tienda (la)	shop, store
tú	you (*sing. informal*)
tú tienes	you have

V

vaca (la)	cow
vegetal (el)	vegetable
vehículo (el)	vehicle
venado (el)	deer
ver	to see
verde	green
viaje (el)	trip
viernes	Friday
violeta	purple
volante (el)	steering wheel

Y

yo	I
yo tengo	I have

Z

zoológico (el)	zoo

English–Spanish

A

airplane — *el avión*
alphabet — *el alfabeto*
animal — *el animal* (pl. *los animales*)
antenna — *la antena*
to applaud — *aplaudir*
 Applaud! — *¡Aplaudan!*
arm — *el brazo*

B

back — *atrás*
to be — *ser*
 I am — *yo soy*
 you are — *tú eres* (sing.); *ustedes son* (pl.)
 it's — *eso/esto es*
 to be called — *llamarse*
bear — *el oso*
beautiful, pretty — *bello(a)* (pl. *bellos, bellas*)
big — *grande*
bird — *el pájaro*
black — *negro(a)*
blinker — *intermitente*
blue — *azul*
boat — *el barco*
book — *el libro*
boring — *aburrido(a)*
boy — *el niño*
brother — *el hermano*
brown — *marrón* (pl. *marrones*)
bus — *el autobús*
by — *por*

C

cake — *el pastel*
car — *el coche*
cassette — *la cinta*
city — *la ciudad*
coin — *la moneda*
color — *el color*
cow — *la vaca*

D

dad — *papá*
to dance — *bailar*
 Dance! — *¡Baila!*
day — *el día*
deer — *el venado*
desert — *el desierto*
dessert — *el postre*
direction — *la dirección*
dish — *el plato*
dog — *el perro*
door — *la puerta*

E

eagle — *el águila*
to eat — *comer*
engine — *el motor*

F

family — *la familia*
fast — *rápido*
fast-food — *fast-food*
forest — *el bosque*
Friday — *viernes*
fruit — *la fruta*
fun — *divertido(a)*

G

game — *el juego* (pl. *los juegos*)
 video game — *el juego de video* (pl. *los juegos de video*)
girl — *la niña*
to go — *ir*
 Let's go! — *¡Vamos!*
 to go back — *retroceder*
 Go back! — *¡Retrocede!*
 to go forward — *adelantar/ir adelante*
 Go forward! — *¡Adelante!*
 to go on a trip — *viajar*
good morning/afternoon — *buenos días/tardes*
green — *verde*
gray — *gris*

H

handkerchief — *el pañuelo*
hat — *el sombrero* (pl. *los sombreros*)
to have — *tener*
 I have — *yo tengo*
 you have — *tú tienes*
he, it *(m.)* — *él*
headlights — *las luces*
hello — *hola*
horse — *el caballo* (pl. *los caballos*)
hotel — *el hotel*
house, home — *la casa*
hunger — *el hambre*
 to be hungry — *tener hambre*

I

I — *yo*
ice cream — *el helado*
if — *si*
 if I were . . . — *si yo fuera . . .*
in — *en*
it's — *esto/eso es*

J

to jump — *saltar*
 Jump! — *¡Salta!*
jungle — *la selva*

L

left — *la izquierda*
 to the left — *a la izquierda*
leg — *la pierna*
lion — *el león*
I like . . . — *Me gusta . . .*
long — *largo(a)*
to love — *amar*

M

map — *el mapa*
meat — *la carne*
mom — *mamá*
Monday — *lunes*
mountain — *la montaña*
My name is . . . — *Me llamo . . .*

N

nature — *la naturaleza*
no — *no*

O

ocean — *el océano*
odd — *raro*
orange — *la naranja* (pl. *las naranjas*)

P

park — *el parque*
to pass (another car) — *pasar*
pen — *la pluma*
pink — *rosado(a)*
purple — *violeta*
to put — *poner*
 to put on the blinker — *poner las luces intermitentes*
 I put — *yo puse*

R

to raise — *levantar*
 Raise your arm! — *¡Levanta el brazo!*
 Raise your leg! — *¡Levanta la pierna!*
red — *rojo(a)*
right — *la derecha*
 to the right — *a la derecha*

S

Saturday — *sábado*
to say — *decir*
 I say — *digo*
 "Simon says . . ." — *"Simón dice . . ."*
school — *la escuela*
to see — *ver*
 I see — *veo*
shark — *el tiburón*
she, it *(f.)* — *ella*
sheep — *la oveja*

shop, store	*la tienda*
short	*corto (a)*
to sing	*cantar*
I sing	*canto*
singer	*el cantante* (m.); *la cantante* (f.)
sister	*la hermana*
slow	*lento(a)*
to slow down	*reducir la marcha/ ir más lento*
I slow down	*reduzco la marcha/voy más lento*
you slow down	*tú reduces la marcha/vas más lento*
small	*pequeño(a)*
snake	*la serpiente, la culebra*
something	*algo*
song	*la canción*
to start	*comenzar*
that starts with . . .	*que comienza por . . .*
steering wheel	*el volante*
to stop	*parar*
I stop	*paro*
you stop	*tú paras*
straight	*derecho*
straight ahead	*adelante*
strange	*extraño*
Sunday	*domingo*
sunglasses	*los lentes de sol*
swimming pool	*la piscina*

T

tall	*alto(a)*
taxi	*el taxi*
that	*que*
they *(f.)*	*ellas*
they *(m.)*	*ellos*
Thursday	*jueves*
today	*hoy*
today is . . .	*hoy es . . .*
toy	*el juguete*
treasure	*el tesoro*
tree	*el árbol*
trip	*el viaje*
truck	*el camión*
Tuesday	*martes*
to turn	*dar la vuelta*
Turn!	*¡Dén la vuelta!*
to make a turn	*voltear/doblar*
I make a turn	*yo doblé*

U

ugly	*feo(a)*

V

vegetable	*vegetales*
vehicle	*el vehículo*
video game	*el juego de video* (pl. *los juegos de video)*

W

to walk	*caminar*
Walk!	*¡Camina!(tú), ¡Caminen! (ustedes)*
we	*nosotros*
Wednesday	*miércoles*
week	*la semana*
wheel	*la rueda*
white	*blanco(a)*
who	*quien*

Y

yellow	*amarillo(a)*
yes	*sí*
you	*ustedes/usted* (pl./ sing. formal), *tú* (sing. informal)

Z

zoo	*el zoológico*